A Call From Beyond

Edited by

CHRIS WALTON

First published in Great Britain in 1998 by
TRIUMPH HOUSE
1-2 Wainman Road, Woodston,
Peterborough, PE2 7BU
Telephone (01733) 230749

All Rights Reserved

Copyright Contributors 1998

HB ISBN 1 86161 273 7
SB ISBN 1 86161 278 8

Foreword

More and more people are writing poetry, and using it as a way of communication; sending words of comfort to loved ones, or sharing their feelings with the world.

A Call From Beyond is a special anthology of poetry that contains the thoughts, feelings and emotions of over 90 new and established writers. They have joined hands to share with you a collection of some of the most inspirational work that is being written today.

The poetry in both style and content is as varied as the writers who have contributed, but together they have created a complementary collection that can be enjoyed time and time again.

Chris Walton
Editor

CONTENTS

Moments In Egypt	Iris Metcalfe	1
Wake Up In The Morning	Emily Macintosh	2
Beyond This Horizon	William Hayles	3
Renascent	Gail Susan Halstead	4
Space Travel	Margaret Robinson	5
Space	Judith Pryor	6
The Journey	Richard Cole	7
All Of Them Have Died	John Christopher	8
Hunger	Anne Green	9
The Romanian Round, Winter And Summer 1989	Joanna Watson	10
Beyond The Horizon	Don Goodwin	11
The Man From The Water Board	Robin Lloyd	12
Ireland '97	Anna King	13
Malawi	Teresina N Fullard	14
On Angels' Wings	Irene Dalzell	15
Satan's World	Sarah Hitchens	16
Hotel Keys, A Memory Of Ostende	Kate Fell	17
Well Beyond The Horizon	Keith L Powell	18
Singing In Sarajevo	John Summerville-Binks	19
Daydream	T B Smith	20
Russia/The Downfall	Ann Grimwood	21
Hadrian's Wall	Rita Douglas	22
Limbo	Juliet C Eaton	23
Am I The Alien?	Anita Messer	24
St Valery En Caux 1940	L J Montgomery	25
Flying Pigs	Cath Simpkins	26
From A Sussex Shore	José Morgan	27
Life In Perspective	F E Cove	28
As The Years Pass	E W Eyden	29
Beyond Sense	Irene Munro	30
A Little Science Friction	I White	31
Consider Ants	Ray Talus	32
Vision Of Peace	John Clarke	33
Untitled	Lynda Hippsley	34

Dreams	Elizabeth Fennell	35
Life Goes On	Amanda Jayne Biro	36
The Gift	Catherine Reay	37
The Cry In The Night	Philip Nugent	38
Beyond	D W Fincham	39
Search	Andrea Noelle Vaughan	40
Dolores	L A Churchill	41
In The Firing Line	S Vickers	42
All Heaven In Sight	Margaret Willoughby	43
Looking Back	Reg Morris	44
Through A Microscope	Cathy McAree	45
Lost	John Scroggie	46
Horizon Of Riches	David J Hall	47
Daybreak	Ian Proctor	48
Innocent	Kevin Doc Ryan	49
Nature's Victim	Alison Hulme	50
Untitled	R Dhillion	52
I Came And I Was Conquered	Peter Gledhill	53
Somalia	S K Haddad	54
Undisciplined Drivers	Hilary Jill Robson	55
Monsoon	Rosemary Muncie	56
African Sanctus	Steve Newbury	57
Woman Of Inishmaan	Deirdre Armes Smith	58
South Africa	Emma Knight	59
By Night Train To Nairobi Athi Plain	Joyce Barton	60
Beyond The Horizon	Mary Frances Mooney	61
The Chernobyl Disaster	Sally Ann Swain	62
Grumble	Jenny Bosworth	63
Beyond The Horizon Of Life!	Sheila Olivia Hogan	64
Face At The Window	Pauline Hamblin	65
Armageddon - Beyond The Horizon	B M Hurll	66
The Voice Of Famine	S Y Lee	67
Beyond The Horizon	Patricia Aboagye	68
Lancelot's Pain	Paul Birkitt	69
The Staithes	Chris Bailey	70
Strange Land	P Williams	72

A Transient Experience	Shaun Kelley	73
Sage Of The Sunset	Pamela Harvey	74
Homeless	Kerry D Beck	75
Beyond Question?	D Glossop	76
Outer Space?	Margareth	77
The Daily Routine	Kim Montia	78
God Knows	K M Clemo	79
Hiding From Conflict	E Francis	80
Reaching For Perfection	Peter Corbett	81
Death For A Tusk	Phoenix Martin	82
Dartmoor Prison (Beneath Your Mist)	Norman Royal	83
To Be Another Life Form	Ann G Wallace	84
From The Desert	Alasdair Aston	85
Come Be Set Free	Lesley J Worrall	86
Once And Forever	Dorothea Gray	88
Liberation	Suzanne Joy Golding	89
Untitled	Katy Plant	90
The Gathering	Luke Thomas	91
Living Amonst The Land Mines	C Beodricksworth Reynolds	92
Nia-Tama's Children - Rwanda	Antony Gilbert	93
The Spririt Within	Paul Wadge	94
Afternoon Tea	M C Taylor	95
Space	B Clarke	96
Nutrition For Yashoda	Maureen Macnaughtan	97
Bexhill Streets After School	Gillian C Fisher	98
Blinded By The Light	Sonia Conway	99

MOMENTS IN EGYPT

From Luxor, where the famous temples stand,
We toured the tombs where once the pharaohs lay.
Our guide was known as best in all the land
And held us spellbound while he showed the way.

With tales of ancient gods and kings he led
Our little party down beneath the ground.
The words inscribed upon the walls he read
While we surveyed the paintings all around.

And soon the wall before me seemed to fade,
The painted figures stirred and moved about.
I watched the workers when the tombs were made,
And moving closer heard them laugh and shout.

Then rousing fanfares blown upon a horn
Grew louder still as marching columns neared,
And shoulder-high upon a litter borne
The pharaoh in his robes of state appeared.

The vivid daydream blurred and then was gone.
The painted scenes were back upon the wall.
The little group had started moving on;
There was no other movement there at all.

Iris Metcalfe

WAKE UP IN THE MORNING

Wake up in the morning,
Ring a bell.
Room service,
Like a hotel.
Wake up in the morning,
Feeling down low.
Laying beside a
Shop window.
Wake up in the morning,
High up in a tree.
Chattering to your mother,
'Come and feed me.'
Wake up in the morning,
Grumpy or gay.
Whatever you are,
Start a fresh new day.

Emily Macintosh (10)

BEYOND THIS HORIZON

Beyond this horizon my eyes can see,
In future times before hope fails,
A land where my children can walk free,
Liberation for my beloved Wales.

When the English yoke shall be broken,
and the heathen driven from our land,
When in pride the Welsh is spoken,
and peace and love walk hand in hand.

When saints like David, Samson and more,
and mighty heroes of Llewellyn's line,
Pray to God, our faith to restore,
and hope that he shall send a sign.

Where bards can sing of valour again.
While children gather at their knee,
Where God in glory once more to reign
From Offa's dyke to the open sea.

Beyond this horizon my eyes can see,
A golden age bathed in heaven's light,
Hurry now, my Lord to me,
Guide me through the darkest night.

The Celtic cross bears Jesus' pain,
The circle shows our unity,
In patient waiting our hearts remain,
Till beyond this horizon our Lord we see.

William Hayles

RENASCENT

The bright light is calling out to me,
Do I answer its call?
Beyond the horizon what will there be?
If I answer they'll take my soul.

After the horizon I was aiming for,
There was another to take its place.
I look closely, is that a door?
I'm sure I saw a familiar face!

I now see friends, long since demised,
Are they reaching out to me?
I see serenity, in their eyes,
Only their holiness, I can see.

My new horizon is growing nearer,
I wonder what I'll leave?
Present fading, the light is clearer,
My family, I don't want to grieve.

I enter the light, friends are waiting,
Are they to be my guides?
The calmness, is almost sedating,
My soul I give, nothing to hide.

Many more horizons I will meet,
As I travel beyond and on.
This heavenly bliss, you cannot beat,
My last horizon dead and gone.

Gail Susan Halstead

SPACE TRAVEL

I was searching for the truth
Through my own tears.
Staring blindly into space
At the outer atmosphere.
Rocket motors roaring past
To the moon, there to despatch.
Logging everything in sight
Systems guided, light-planed.
Travelled in a starless night
Alone again in a clear blue sky.
I was searching for the truth
Strawberry eyes have past.

Margaret Robinson

Space

I've only recently started watching the Roddenbury soap,
Which is based in he 25th century to give us all hope,
For a future of travel by any means,
With all kinds of aliens with varying genes.

They travel for years in just a matter of seconds,
Go from planet to planet wherever trouble beckons;
But our heroes don't get hurt as they travel life's road,
'Cos they live by truth and justice, with an honour code.

There's Carassians, Bagjorans and Changelings at work,
Meeting Pickard, Sisko, Janeway and Kirk,
They have Dax and Kira for eye appeal,
With Worf and Chakote giving an alien feel.

Each week we travel at warp in outer space,
With the Federation keeping peace all over the place
If you've not guessed by now what this is called,
Then you're not a Trecker - I'm appalled!

Judith Pryor

THE JOURNEY

Do not think I am gone. I am but a few steps
Before you, walking home.
I leave you not alone,
But with my love, whilst I
Prepare my home for you.
There, I'll place robes on you;
Place sandals on your feet.
And then, you too, are home.

Do not think I am gone.
Think of me, and I am
There with you; in your thoughts.
Dream of me, and I am
There, walking beside you.
Love me, and I am there:
Hand in hand; heart in heart
You do not know where my
Heart begins, or where yours ends.
My hand is yours; yours is mine:
One in one. Love in love.

So, do not think I am gone
For, in you I am;
In you, I stay.

Richard Cole

ALL OF THEM HAVE DIED!

They cannot get to shops and stores.
There is no food to buy,
and all the clothes they have, they wear
as on the earth they lie.

There is no home to call their own,
except the barren ground.
There is no laughter in their hearts
for only tears are found.

They have no toys. No books to read.
Nothing to entertain,
and often all their hopes and dreams
lie in a drop of rain.

Their cherished friends are lying down
and sometimes never rise,
and all the pain of helplessness
is etched in dying eyes.

Don't talk to them of faithfulness.
What is there to believe,
when this next moment of today
may be the last they breathe?

Who thinks of justice for each soul?
Who gives each one a chance?
The world has got no need of them
and barely spares a glance.

Have you sat down and thought of them?
My friend, have you once cried?
Too late. Tomorrow is too late
for all of them have died!

John Christopher

HUNGER

Hunger stares out
of an empty bowl
with dark, hollow eyes
that enters one's soul.

Young flesh
hangs as an overcoat
on a skeleton frame.
Alive yet frozen
in a vacant age.

Small stomachs
stretch to a fullness
appearing as a mirage
in a barren land.

Death comes as an imaginary friend,
beckons and smiles
to hunger . . . that has no end.

Anne Green

THE ROMANIAN ROUND, WINTER AND SUMMER 1989
(Mămăligă is a traditional Romanian dish of stodgy maize-meal porridge)

Like mămăligă. Torpid queues: ice feet
on sallow matchsticks blanching in the street,
awaiting news of possible supplies;
blenched fears of stepping out of line, of Eyes
and Ears, decreasing rations . . . Shops now leached

of protein, stuffed with paper noodles; meat
three times a year, perhaps . . . Just scraps to eat:
embalmed tomatoes, cardboard bread and lies
like mămăligă.

Then passive queues like serpents in the heat,
scorched blades of grass, unbending stalks of wheat:
await a crowded trolley-bus; arise
at two for milk; pay bills; seek food, replies,
a pair of shoes . . . Such nothing hours, each feat
like mămăligă.

Joanna Watson

BEYOND THE HORIZON

Beyond the horizon far into space.
Beyond the eye of the human race.
Is a place beyond all imagination.
Yet it still holds man's fascination.
It is a land where time don't dwell.
It's quite the opposite of hell.
No-one can see it until they die.
I can hear you now asking me why?
If you could see that land today.
You'd want to be now on your way.
Alas you have a certain time here on earth.
Before you can have that second birth.

Don Goodwin

The Man From The Water Board

For a while no-one breathed.
The gases condensed into oceans.
Earth hissed. The land boiled.
Only the stars looked down.

The man from the Water Board
came and took samples. When he
returned there was a starfish,
confirming his findings.

For a while everything (it seemed) breathed.
The oceans were full of fish.
Earth sprouted cities. People let off steam.
The stars still looked down.

The man from the Water Board
returned for his routine check.
Earth hissed. The land boiled.
It was the umpteenth time. He was fed up.

But he took his samples, grumbling that
he wouldn't be sorry if this were the last time.

Robin Lloyd

IRELAND '97

The women came out in the morning
The horror they see at dawn.
In silence they stand outside
Despair can be seen in their eyes.
The sun shines with a warm glow
Exposing the dreadful show.
All night the terror went on
Shouts and screams from the awful throng.
Now they have all gone home
Leaving those streets alone,
They will probably be back tonight
Can you remember why they fight?

Anna King

Malawi

Around me was beauty, the gardens were green.
The flowers were vibrant, the most lovely I'd seen.
But out of the garden and around to the back,
In the corner of the yard was a little shack.
To us it's a hovel, to him it was home.
We can't understand how it's the best that he'd known.
But that's how life is, when you go to that place.
The rich live by money, the poor live by grace.

And now far away from the scenes that were there,
As I idly sit in my fireside chair.
I cannot forget the warmth that I miss,
Of a people, whose country to me did not exist.
They have so much more than we have to give,
I will never forget as long as I live.
Of families who'd camp in hospital grounds,
So they didn't leave loved ones, to be on their own.

Cool balmy nights and hot dusty days,
Waking at dawn is just one of their ways.
When Sunday comes, there's no time for a rest,
Because everyone gets dressed, in their very best.
Mud hut villages throughout the nation,
Beautiful churches built, to the God of creation.
A share in the beauty of all that they see,
Is the wonderful gift, that they gave to me.

Teresina N Fullard

ON ANGELS' WINGS

A new day dawns . . . the sunrise smiles
yet darkness lingers with all its wiles
unseen but so real and near
. . . unwelcome to the peace we seek
but we are told to never fear
yet these wiles like lions' jaws are too near
do not disappear . . . but in devious disguise
they mark their mile with such wicked guile
to prey like beasts without soul
murdering goodness their only goal!
Even ignore new babies' breath so pure
and too beautiful for their minds so blind . . .
so do we flee on angels' wings to be free!

Free from searching still for peace
because reality does not cease
. . . in lands far and near man flees foe in fear!
Terror stalks its prey which prays to be free
amidst this gallery of fear menacingly near
in such disguise to innocent eyes
which plead in vain to be free
from tiring tirade where dreams all fade . . .
crushed by a world without care
and a world of war . . . like a beast's huge jaw
in all its disguise which ravage and gnaw
each and all . . . fragile and frail
innocents driven from their homes and shore
denied all love . . . can peace be no more?
Hope is for all . . . that man one day will be free
from beasts in disguise with wiles behind smiles
Oh on angels' wings may we be free!

Irene Dalzell

Satan's World

Through the eye of my dreams,
I witness what was once a secret paradise.
In the land of slaughtering skies,
Where the devil takes flight.
Outside the sinners' gate,
He towers over me with his desire to possess.
My overwhelming imagination
Leaves me trapped within my mind.
He longs to possess my inner soul
And hold me as a prisoner of hate,
Fill me with evil and death,
And thoughts that are endured by pain.
Devil worshippers on the road to nowhere,
Live and breathe for this evil grim giant.
I long to be free,
Away from those who are naturally bad,
Where I am protected from harm
And shielded from that devilsome world.

Sarah Hitchens

HOTEL KEYS, A MEMORY OF OSTENDE
(A true story)

Tabs on keys, with numbers printed, for hotel rooms, we're all aware,
But cross the sea, and no-one's hinted, the sort you'll find whilst over there!
Not content with numbered disc, on key to room, it's not so good -
They bored a hole, then tied with string, a hefty awkward piece of wood!
Handbag was large, so took the key, and passed the desk that morning,
But Madame was mad, and let me know, when I returned - a warning!
The key must be returned to desk, on each farewell occasion!
But as to why, the lady gave not any explanation!
The reason must be very strong, to merit desperate measures!
Hotel next-door, with keys galore, hung coconuts on their treasures!
Perhaps they're afraid, if you take the key, you'll pass it on to others,
To use as they will, or borrow the bed, and share it with their brothers!

Kate Fell

WELL BEYOND THE HORIZON

Well beyond the horizon I want to be
In Texas with my horse, gun and me
Among the trails of the old west
Who have not caught up with the modern times just yet.

Well beyond the horizon I want to be
In Paris, France I long to be
Young and in love without a care
The pick of new things always to wear.

Well beyond the horizon I want to be
Either back in time or forward you see
For this time I just don't like
And want it well out of my sight.

Keith L Powell

SINGING IN SARAJEVO

The sun has left us here in Sarajevo.
Grey cases lie disused - smoking,
As I walk through the pallid streets of death.
A lack of grass here now - a football match
Takes place where the hospital once stood;
Their footsteps cast sharply in the sunless grey talc.

This is a contemporary hell they are in,
The authorities enforce -
There are no Sarajevo - Samaritans
In this ever-increasing grey curtain of death.
The people have suffered a black-leaded obliteration,
Their homes have opened up, swallowing them into
A black-hole of continual despair - a murky misery.

Blackness descends - the green hills enmeshed,
As the angry array of the dead artillery are
Overshadowed momentarily -
But the black keeps them there.
Here, we are all prisoners in this drab domain;
We cannot live, we cannot breathe - suffocating,
As we sing for Sarajevo.

John Summerville-Binks

DAYDREAM

As I lie here in bed, waiting
For the caring people to help me,
I remember what the world was like,
When there was a time I walked.
I wonder what my life would be like
If I hadn't had that crash.
Found that lover, become a mother,
Succeeded in nursing,
Found friends, travelled the world,
Explored the unexplored, met the oppressed,
Treated the starving, helped the wounded,
Learned what life is really like?
Just to walk and run is a dream,
To read as I could twenty years ago.
(An eye nerve damaged so partly blind.)
Just to see the world as others do,
To enjoy the colours of the rainbow,
While I think of this magic word 'beyond'
I realise I'm better off in some ways
But in others not - it's unbelievable.

T B Smith

RUSSIA/THE DOWNFALL

Long queues waiting, for something not worth having
They clamber over each other to get the best
Young and old standing together, bonded only by their need for food
Unhappiness lingering in the air, like a storm cloud ready to erupt
Extortionate prices for meat weeks old, the putrid smell hanging in the air
Government not interested in the need of their people
Sitting getting fat on the money, maybe things will change
Maybe things will get better, we can only live in hope.

Ann Grimwood

Hadrian's Wall

The wall is still and quiet
It stretches far as the eye can see,
Can we hear the guards whispering?
No ghostly voices haunting thee.

Emperor Hadrian built this wall
To stem the enemy hordes,
Soldiers marching in the silence
Not a sound of clashing swords.

We rest here at Vindolanda
Hundreds of years have past,
No Roman soldiers passing by
Only their shadows in the grass.

Broken stones set in the ground
Once they were Roman rooms,
Now these are only silent mounds
Or maybe ancient tombs.

This wall has stood the test of time,
A memory of Hadrian
Years that come and years that go,
Into the great Millennium.

Rita Douglas

LIMBO

Dancing on a cloud of freedom
Dancing with eternal joy
Where the earthly voice of passion
Cannot e'er the soul destroy
Looking backwards to the future
Looking forward to the past
Rhythmic time now lost in wonder
Where life's pendulum halts at last.
Many decades stand in limbo
Centuries or only weeks.
Who can see the past or future
No-one knows and no-one seeks
Dancing on a cloud of mystery
Drifting through eternal void
Gone all pain and thirst or hunger
Wrapped in peace and overjoyed
Rhythmic time so lost in wonder
Where and when is journey's end
But this is not ours to ponder
We will go where time will send.

Juliet C Eaton

AM I THE ALIEN?

Wandering around space at a lonely hour,
I feel the universe and its limitless power.
I look beyond my judgement, look beyond crime,
and I see beyond the boundaries of time.

My destiny and goals are timeless.
My intention out here is harmless.
This spaceship is my womb, the universe my mother.
The stars are my sisters, the planets my brothers.

All to see is like the boundaries of my mind.
Mine to discover and mine to find.
I am so excited, and yet have endless fear.
One soulful minute, so alien to a year.

As I travel along, alas I ignore earth.
With its chaos and continuous birth.
It has such anger and endless turmoil.
with its continuous weight of crumbling soil.

For I landed there once to help and wave,
I ended up being prodded and labelled, not saved.
Me, I was feared? Hurt and abused,
So I left there battered and confused.

The people didn't outwardly see they,
hadn't really discovered anything that way.
For was the one who had escaped, I was free.
For I was alien to them, but they certainly were
                                    to me.

Anita Messer

ST VALERY EN CAUX 1940

That night they turned toward the battle length
They had no heed, nor sought self-pity then.
Somewhere life passed in brilliance, other men
Danced and wined with sweethearts. Used their strength
In all the fine delights of natural youth.
They who had known these moments did not weep
Nor yet the spirit bruised with empty bitterness.
Worlds are built by blood and their distress
Was at its hour endured. Man is deep
And will pursue unendingly his truth.
If nothing counts that all their monstrous pain
Was worn but to defeat. Whoever shares
Belief in any value man reveres
Will to these men accord eternal gain.

L J Montgomery

FLYING PIGS

Seeing my name in print
sends shivers down my spine,
to be endowed and endorsed with a penguin
beneath would be just fine.

Lassoing small press publishers
from a bulging list.
Fat pile of optimistic beginnings
ready for the post.

Potential publishers for my pearls
ever hopeful belief in flying pigs.

I lust for an ISBN
I dream on and fantasise
about those flying pigs zooming before my eyes.

Who to dedicate to,
the splendid isolation of my name on a titled page.
Which publisher will be my Prints Charming?
To have blood on my axe, my first kill,
a thrill.

Publish and be damned
or darned if not published,
hole in my life.

'Not heard of *her*,
she's a Faber-less poet.'

Cath Simpkins

FROM A SUSSEX SHORE

They will not rise again, those Saxon kings
To chase the Norse invader from their door.
Eternal sleep enfolds them in her wings
and rocks them as the sea erodes the shore.
Where the transient shingle ebbs and flows,
Horned-poppy and Sea Holly, seeds and grows.

They will not draw a sword nor raise a spear,
though Clouded Yellows swarm; a saffron shroud
and quaking grass reiterates our fear
that Europe is too brusque, too louche, too proud.
Forlorn, Canute's wraith, haunts this reclaimed land,
aware our time is but a grain of sand.

José Morgan

LIFE IN PERSPECTIVE

One more day upon this land
Then homeward-bound we go
No more strolling on the sand
Just crunching on the snow
It's nice to escape to exotic plains
And capture all the sights
But lovely to return again
And sleep on cooler nights
At some point in our time of life
We all need to regress
Away from all the stress and strife
Ones left, we love no less
As I look from our balcony
I'll memorise this day
The sight of the blue twinkling sea
The cat that's just a stray
The distant wail and call to prayer
For Muslims to attend
The darkness of the Asian hair
The Chinese/Indian blend
So onto a big aeroplane
The giant bird of the sky
To move back in the faster lane
But how long for and why?

F E Cove

AS THE YEARS PASS

Let me dream my dreams of the years that are past,
Years that were filled with loving and laughter,
When life with its binding spell held me fast,
A spell that mocked at thoughts of hereafter.
Let me sigh for the years that stretched ahead,
Years without number their end far away.
Now the passage of time fills me with dread,
The dread of death in the face of decay.
Let me yearn for the life that lies beyond,
The glory beyond the trauma of death.
Life that was sealed with an unbroken bond,
When the Lord of all Life breathed his last breath.
    Let me plead His name, when my course is run,
    To live in Christ through the triumph He won.

E W Eyden

BEYOND SENSE

Beyond sense, she has no clue of time,
No sense of place,
No sense; she doesn't recognise my face.

She likes her smokes; she loves a drink.
She dresses well.
But where her clothes come from, she cannot tell.

She doesn't mention God to me, but
Paints her face.
Some would say her life is just a waste.

I overhear the reasoned ones to say
What is the point?
They'd say there's more brains in a ruminant!

But in senility's unlikely cloister,
She heard His call.
She had a touch from God - that's all.

She woke from sleep - she dreamt of God - she said
With great conviction.
Thank God, His love knows no restriction.

'I've been touched,' is what she said to me.
No, not deluded!
But in God's family she's now included.

The smart, all health and wealth may have
No sense of grace.
No sense! They do not recognise His face.

Not like the lepers and the blind and deaf, this soul -
They all seemed odd.
Beyond our reach, though all were touched by God.

Irene Munro

A Little Science Friction

'Is there anybody there?' said the radio-astronomer,
Knocking on the starlit night.
The answer - an enigmatic crackle of static -
Wasn't what he'd hoped for, quite.

Very frustrating!
And that pulsar, NGX555
Tells you nothing very constructive;
Just carries on blandly pulsating.
And black holes, for all their popular fame, are the same -
Keep everything to themselves!

'Ah well, then,' the radio-astronomer said,
I'll try once again, then I'm off to bed.'

Meanwhile, high overhead
(Unseen while he was getting frustrated)
The wandering ashes of a star
Had streaked the night with tiny fire;
A star, moreover (though little does he know,
Our astronomer with his radio)
Which became a supernova
Some twenty million years ago, or thereabouts,
Obliterating its attendant satellites,
Where dwelt extraordinary beings, of whom,
After unimaginable journeyings,
An atomised residuum
Is now very near, is here,
Is falling, falling down the atmosphere.

'There's nothing there,' the radio-astronomer said,
'I've had enough!'
And later, as he undressed for bed,
He flicked a fleck of stardust from his cuff.

I White

CONSIDER ANTS

Consider ants; no less no more
And if you will, or if you care
Project yourself, grand conqueror
Of lesser things, and be aware
That you, and they, may juxtapose
The states of being, reason knows

But reason knows no common cause
As mortals testify; as time
Or circumstance gives room for pause
Considering the crass, sublime
Irrelevance, of large and small
In truth, of no real note at all

Watch, as the creature, and its band
Conspires to lift and move a leaf
Along a path, unswerving, and
Heads nestward-bound; in sharp relief
To humans, caught in disarray
Unsure of meaning to their day

No ant can ever contemplate
So large a being as a man
Instead, it must pursue its fate
Task-oriented, in a plan
Which owes its being to the whole
The stuff of life-form protocol

Then halt, before you play at God
And stamp the creature in the dust
Or, leastways, think the notion odd
In all respects, if stamp you must
For greater beings we can't see
Could treat us, thus, unequally

Ray Talus

VISION OF PEACE
(Dedicated to the children who are victims of this world's insincerity)

I have this vision of peace, set in this land
where children play among the flowering fields,
To see their smiling faces, a vision so grand
their laughter like the tinkling of bells pealed.

Would'st not those who died and suffered
have been given this, a life of joy and fun,
But for man's greed and foolish hatred
denied those young souls this vision with the gun.

Tranquil life could be for those who old in years,
their vision, is it of peace or one of hope,
Does memory of days gone by end in tears
or does happiness come with wisdom to cope.

I see my vision of peace in the hearts of men
who will hear the message of their children,
When the look in their eyes says please daddy
make for me a life in a world that is happy.

John Clarke

UNTITLED

Problems amount across the land
But with you Lord
They walk hand in hand
Hardship is among them
Trouble and strife
But it's you O Lord
They'll follow for life
And though their faith may cause them harm
They know they're safe within your arms

Lynda Hippsley

DREAMS

With longing eyes I gaze across
At islands in the sun,
With rocky cliffs and sea-washed shores
White, where the breakers run.

Like jewels in a shimmering sea
With other treasurers stored.
Those lovely islands beckon me
Mysterious, unexplained.

In dreams I walk those distant shores
But look back constantly,
To places known and loved before
So safe, so dear to me.

But then I wake and I am back
Upon this sunlit shore,
Where foaming waves swirl round my feet
And sea birds swoop and soar.

But now, it's time for me to leave
And cross that shimmering sea,
Discover inner isles of peace
Make dreams reality.

Elizabeth Fennell

LIFE GOES ON

Some say it's fate that one day you'll reach heaven's gate.
When your life is completed and the past is deleted.
Only your soul remains from the years of joy and pain.
Since the chains set you free, to rest in the gardens of tranquillity.
Where flowers grow and the streams gently flow.
The birds sing and love is everything.
Then one day you'll return to the before, when life calls once more.
To it's lonely shore within it's open door.
Where you'll start anew, like a child of innocence so pure and true.

Amanda Jayne Biro

THE GIFT

If I should die don't bury me
In regimented cemetery.
But lay me in the open ground
With woods and birdsong all around.

Then plant a tree above my bed
And let it by my body be fed
Receive the gift that once was mine,
And there my soul can spend its time.

Catherine Reay

THE CRY IN THE NIGHT

In the grey sky of
the night, the clouds
passed like flying swans
under a milky shining
moon, only the rapid fire
of the guns brought a brighter
sky which shrieked the
stillness from this timeless
scene, the mortar and
the guns cascading
with a lightning glow
only the blood of a tiny body
shaped by the shrapnel
just a mother weeping
in an entombed shell

Innocence has no friend
a cry was all that could be heard
in the grey sky of the night.

Philip Nugent

BEYOND

Where is that country, where the golden place
beyond the fray of fish, the brawl of bird,
the beat of living hearts that must be heard
around the world, far from the human race?

When is that hour, when the golden time
beyond the sky that marks the end of day
with wind and rain, when weary lives decay
and what was said and done is read in rhyme?

Youth need not to care to question or to ask,
consumed with movement, passion and desire,
but, when those years of easy senses fade,
mortal life will be set at last, remade
beyond the earth, beyond the natural fire
of here and now, to harden like a mask.

D W Fincham

SEARCH

I dwell alone in deepest space,
Of others true there is no trace.
Mere words remain of woman, man,
Their meanings vague within my RAM.
The past unclear, but knowledge grown,
My purpose a quest, my self alone,
I drift as gaseous colours torn,
No sight, I see each new star born,
Nutrinos dart from every source,
The comet blazing on its course.
No touch but sense the solar storm,
The mighty billowing galaxies form,
The matter on the other side
Beyond this universe divide.
I have no sad or happy mien,
No sense of time, no goal or dream
But to explore in smallest states
The molecules of matter's traits.
Still now I find within my whole
A different sort, with different role.
I think I made a special form
Unknown before, this helix born
It needs a place that's more than me,
Somewhere to grow, to live, to be,
A planet warmed beside its sun,
My search for life at last is won.

Andrea Noelle Vaughan

DOLORES

Hands clasped close to hide the shivers of age;
man to man he speaks to his son.
'When will you marry?'
He had lived the hardships of his clan;
worked this family plot, and now, before the grey shadows
of the harvest moon he asked the future of his blood.

Times have slipped; his lad grew strong and dark,
clever at his books; quiet, he looked at the
world and showed no fear.
A father's duty sighed. 'It's only fair to tell her,
son, a woman's years for children are fewer than ours.
Let Dolores go, if she is not for you.'

His boy looked at the sad dried earth, the walls so white
they stung his eyes, at the hills of stone, the sky of steel.
'Papa, I cannot.'
The old man heard the dream crack the harsh air;
and said 'Another?'
'I cannot say.' And said it all.

Across four continents this lad had chased his dreams,
escaped, returned so many times;
this marriage was not for him.
'Tell me.' Silence. 'Her name?'
'Her looks?' A sigh. 'Her eyes are blue . . .
she is unusual. I am not sure.'

Uncertainty hung on the breeze. 'Bring her son,
for my blessing, when the time is right.'
'Papa!'
'Dolores; think on her waiting, be fair.'
'How can I be sure?' They paced the
furrowed plot and felt the seasons change.

L A Churchill

In The Firing Line

Many miles away from home
dreaming of places that I know
lost in a nightmare of reality
I repeat to myself
I'm still alive, I'm still alive.

Many miles away from home
cold, hungry and alone
wondering where to turn,
who to trust
whispering to myself
I'm still sane, I'm still sane.

Many miles away from home
dreaming of places that I know
shall I stay or shall I go.
Finding the strength inside, I know
I'm still alive, I'm still alive.

S Vickers

ALL HEAVEN IN SIGHT

The boy in him peeped from the windows
of the old man's eyes
as, with a child's great wonder and surprise,
he saw again his first leaf fall;
felt snowflakes melt in tiny hands
clasped tight;
marvelled at painted butterflies;
striped, furry bees;
held strings of kite and, with amazement
and delight, heeded its soaring flight;
ran, laughing through the puddles in the rain
and gathered from the beach again
bright gems - the fragile shells
and multi-coloured stones -
which sparkle in the sun when tides recede.
Smelled fresh-baked bread;
tasted the first sweet clover-scented honey;
held in his hot and sticky hand
his stick of rock bought with the precious penny
of his pocket money
and, at the end of day, his prayers said,
heard favourite stories read
by his loved parents at his bed.
And so to sleep.
Heaven lay about him still.
Through all his life, whatever came,
he had retained a child's unquenchable delight -
that eager sense of wonder and surprise
which kept all Heaven in sight.

Margaret Willoughby

LOOKING BACK

If we could go back in time to a previous existence
When creatures weird of many types roamed around with us persistence
Although research will show how life on earth was chanced
We'll never really know the facts which are little way romanced
Remains are found of animals which give scientists statistics
And they will always use these facts to satisfy the mystics
For science likes things cut and dried with minimum contradiction
But there is sometimes cause to think that some of it is fiction
It's interesting yet a little frightening to contemplate how things were
There must have been strange animals and birds most everywhere
Just imagine what it was like when the creatures were our neighbours
When hunting for our food each day was a normal part of our labours
There were no superstores or corner shops to supply us with our food
We would have to do the best we could to feed the growing brood
In place of shops barter was a friendly form of trade
When in exchange for some possessions an agreement would be made
There'd be no argas, microwaves or ovens to do our cooking
And there'd be no time to stand and stare for wood we would
Be looking
Then we'd have to rub two sticks in order to produce a flame
It would be a necessity and not as in our day treated as a game
There'd be no such things as saucepans, plates, spoons or knife and fork
And no invention like the telephone but it would still be good to talk
We should stop and wonder what we've gained by being civilised
It may be things that cause most distress are the ones most
often prized
We've choked our road with vehicles which means more and
more pollution
And no one seems to face the facts and have a sensible solution
We're all to blame for many things that have been planned for us
And although we can't go back so far in time to join the brontosaurus
It would be nice if we could go to somewhere in between
Where VAT or income tax were things that had never been.

Reg Morris

THROUGH A MICROSCOPE

I looked into another world
A microscope view of life
The dot I placed upon the slide
Revealed a secret
A God I felt when looking down
This tubular manmade device
For I saw another world
So small, so neat, precise.
Could it be that we
Are being seen as a dot upon a screen
By something in the universe
Earth a unicellular organ
Of a multi-cellular universe
Floating about in space?

Cathy McAree

Lost

Lost in the great snows of the
hidden land, my beings fibre taught
and grand, contemplating every
strand of mystic thought. Dwelling
on eternal sound, clear resonance
and mighty bound the spirits free.

Time carves the path of quiet
meditation, revealing truths of
absolute cosmic speculation.
Natures changed her silent plan,
all encompassing dynamic stand,
the cosmos breathes.

John Scroggie

HORIZON OF RICHES

Life of shear delight
To be able to be rich
No need for many worries
To live in London, keep my flat in Birmingham
To have an apartment in New York
A villa in Spain
To go where you wish
Anytime, anywhere, any place
Dreams of reality
Beyond the horizon
The horizon of dreams
Maybe one day realised
Champagne for breakfast
Unlimited travel
Concorde to New York
Voyage around the world
Travel the Orient Express
Reach beyond the horizon.

David J Hall

DAYBREAK

Daybreak will find me
In a land far away
Where no one will know me
Or care if I stay.
A land of no questions
Where the past lies so deep
A past that's respected
When you've a secret to keep.

Who can I turn to
Or trust in my heart
For I may face tomorrow
Like a fool in the dark?
With nothing to cling to
Or nowhere to go
I'm just like a blind man
Who can't see his foe.

I know that she stumbled
As she fell from the train
They said that I'd killed her
And I took the blame.
For fifteen long years
I've prayed for the day
For an end to this nightmare
And freedom each day.

Daybreak will tell me
If I've got a friend
Or a pact with the devil
Or a road with no end.
I'm looking for something
I can't even see
But I'll know when it happens
For then I'll be free
With someone who really loves me.

Ian Proctor

INNOCENT

She looks for her toy beneath the stairs
But too much rubble and broken chairs
While her mother sleeps, she will not wake
Deaf to the pleas her daughter might make
And why can the sky be seen from here?
This haven shattered letting outside come bare
Yet the morning sky is dark, no more sunlight
Behind the clouds of dust, makes it seem night
When those clouds laden, they shed black rain
Stinging her young eyes, no protecting glass pane;
She still hears the siren that brought the fear
Her mother had cried loud, holding her near
And the picture box now, a burnt out shell
It had proclaimed the wrath of coming hell
The 'powers' had risen, showing their weapons' might
And the warheads were launched into furious flight;
But she is too innocent to 'understand' this hate
How men of greed have decided her fate
Their fear and ignorance was such a sin
To start a war only the worms would win;
So she finds her doll and the sickness grows more
Her skin feels on fire, she slips to the floor
And she closes weary eyes, wishing her mother's embrace
Then finds eternal sleep, no more human race.

Kevin Doc Ryan

NATURE'S VICTIM

My friends don't understand me
and kin, they think I'm strange.
Sometimes I'm just aloof,
and others half deranged.

Folk often stop to ask me,
when will we have a child?
'It's time you thought about it,'
they tell me, with a smile.

Oh, if only I'd a gold coin,
for every time I've cried,
I'd be the richest woman,
but for the child I am denied.

Days and weeks of waiting,
then excited hopes are dashed,
God only knows my heartbreak,
as each month my dreams are smashed.

A miracle conception
is the ultimate of fem,
so 'why am I a victim?'
goes through my mind again.

A busy life I'm leading,
and always in the throng,
but within the constant vacuum,
echoes loudly what is wrong.

The poor, unwanted children,
are they nature's victims too?
I'd love a child if I were blessed;
my dreams begin anew . . .

In my wake I can't forget it,
and it haunts me all night through.
Everywhere I look are babies,
pregnant mums and toddlers too.

So my nightmare is unending,
fate's obsession growing more,
will I ever feel a babe inside,
or loss and pain for evermore.

Alison Hulme

Untitled

Clasp your hands and fly up high
Spread your arms across the skies
Fly around the silver moon, but come down again very soon
Open out your once clasped hands
and shake out all that silver sand
As it falls beneath your feet feel
that sense of light and ease
As it glows around your body
dazzle your eyes with all its beauty.

As your senses they dance as one
the words they fail to come
For the skies that once were darkened
now awake and bathe in brightness
As this wonder seeps slowly outwards
all it touches turns to gladness.

R Dhillion

I Came And I Was Conquered

Alas, I am no Shakespeare! I'm not weak
At Latin and I'm good at Greek.
For fifteen years I laboured to imbibe
The lingos of those long since silenced tribes;
And though I was derided as a swot,
At least I'm not a Saxon monoglot!
Yet ever inspiration failed my pen -
For poems now are not like poems then.
So now Welsh learner classes I attend,
And to the angels' tongue my mind I bend:
Each week I learn new noises, try to spell
Words starting with two d's and double ell.
However heard I swot I never will
Write bardic verse like Dafydd Son of Bill;
But maybe I'll inscribe - and what a promise! -
Good English like the blessed Dylan Thomas.

Peter Gledhill

Somalia

Those walking skeletons, covered with skin,
Exposed in all parts with sores on the shin
Are too young for hair to grow on the chin,
Too lean for death which snatches hundreds in.

Squatting skeletons upon the dry ground,
Motionless and silent, without a sound,
Oblivious that burial pits are found
Cluttered with corpses till their turn comes round.

Exhausted skeletons show no surprise
When their mouths an noses are veiled with flies
That suck the moisture from these and their eyes
As they lie helpless, unable to rise.

We watch them on the television screen
Between food adverts which seem too obscene
With no other record that they have been
A part of this world, stuck in a latrine.

The nations supplied food, and drugs to heal,
But bellies swelled for the lack of a meal
When warring scoundrels continued to steal
And mercy died in hearts structured of steel.

O Lord, speed the time when justice prevails
That food may reach camps, villages and vales,
The land of the vacant mouth and entrails
Where the weak cannot cry when death assails.

S K Haddad

UNDISCIPLINED DRIVERS

Taxiing to hospital
We are in Agra, not the capital,
Transport cumbersome, dated, unfamiliar,
No traffic code here in India.
Vehicles criss-cross highway, this way and that,
Only stop if they break down or for a tyre-flat,
No-one is trapped in an enmesh,
Nothing interferes with this seething mesh.
Gesticulating drivers, ill-tempered, grumpy,
Roads are churned up, dusty, bumpy,
Several carts ambling, bumbling; oxen-drawn,
Motorists with fingers permanently on the horn.
No traffic lights or rights of way,
But directing this ants nest every day,
Standing on a rostrum, gun and truncheon-armed cop,
White gloved hands signalling, non-stop.
Owners of lorries, trucks, ringing handbells,
Off-side and near-side wings dented, cracked like eggshells,
Cycle rickshaws, cheap runabout,
A policeman stops one, argues, then hand clouts
Several times around the head, know not what about!
Foreign passengers expressing doubt,
Apparently wishing they could get out.
Only the sacred cow is shown great love and care,
Detouring her on the thoroughfare,
Allowed to roam and wander aimlessly,
To do as she wishes quite unreservedly.
Pinch myself! Am I in a talkie
Of Keystone Kops film and no-one's told me?

Hilary Jill Robson

MONSOON

Unconcerned the small figure
Crosses a narrow path cutting wet plots
The young rice will be the colour of an emerald
The earth treader reflected in the watery fields
Along with fat clouds rolling high
And their slower pace. Two of him there.
Who chose his lungi of deepest rust?
And on his head a silver pitcher
Catches the sun
Delicate and solitary
The thin figure crosses the paddy fields
Boy carrying a vessel
Rust and silver and jewel green
Above and below the big sky follows.

Rosemary Muncie

African Sanctus

Black edged, grey shrouded pyramids
leaning into the mustard, grit blown day.
Silhouetted minarets stab the yellowed, crimson sky
of dawning,
melts the mullahs cry, icy clear across the sands,
call the faithful, crowded in the dusty streets,
flock like teeming goats to
murmur in the sunrise.

Slap of sandal upon stone,
like fresh fish landed upon a quay,
huddled in their shoals, goaded by ululation
shark circling the reef of houses
to beat upon the temple shore.

Call the faithful - mahdi and domel,
meeting in kehl - mashiek,
eager for their God.
But still, the patient camel stands,
spit chewing, aloof to ro-bed gathering,
where the sands disbelieve the seas existence
and the copper beaten sun slams its dune topped anvil.

Steve Newbury

WOMAN OF INISHMAAN
(Inishmaan is a lonely island off the west coast of Ireland)

Little new child
don't look at me with your milky eyes
that tighten the muscles of my womb
so painfully.
I must harden myself against you.

Lie in your wooden crib
away from my arms
and from the breast
already aching with your loss.

If you had been a girl
I could have kept you longer
but your brothers are calling you
from the pounding waves.
It was for the raging appetite of the sea
that I raised you.

Little new boy
don't search my face for unconditional love!
We have to live on this bare island as best we can.
I will feed you, clothe you,
throw turf on the fire to keep you warm,
but spare me the ultimate penalty of motherhood.

Your dangerous journey away from me
as I lay under the oilskins
that hang from the roof, was pain enough.
I have no strength for further partings.

Framed in this narrow window
the famished sea meets the sky
and gulls swirl upwards from it
like scorched paper from a bonfire.

Deirdre Armes Smith

SOUTH AFRICA

Impressions swarm
like bees
over my first breath
in this world.

Gleaming palaces
mystify our senses
as if children
in wonderland.

Playing as kings
we peer fearfully
to Soweto's nest
of sun-baked tin.

Deep contrasts
thrash to reality,
and we, naive,
have been stung.

We travel bare
as empty plains,
share cartoon roads
with workers' feet.

I try to absorb
an awesome varsity,
along with the hate
of black and white.

Lightning
in a dark African sky.
Nature reflects
on a country's pain.

If only, in this world,
such blazing beauty
could cure every soul.

Emma Knight

By Night Train To Nairobi Athi Plain

Heavily I lay and brooded on a fancied mannered slight,
As the coal-sucked engine jerked us rhythmically across the night,
Till my clammy nape aroused me and I rose distressed, unslept,
Threw the window down and saw what company the carriage kept.
Followed us a lovely lantern, lit our track athwart the plain,
Dimmed the tropic stars, and with her glow washed faint the milky wain:
Lady moon, nor lovelier a lady have I ever seen
Graciously bestowing glory by her contact, as a queen.
All below, the thorns and grasses borrowed beauty out of time -
Once before, in northern winter, did I see the like, in rime;
Not their own, the vivid etchings; given by grace, each silhouette,
Every shifting square uncovered there another picture yet.
More than beauty, 'twas the spirit of that breathless plain I drew,
Here lay time untampered, ages no man ever knew.
Old as Eden, aye and older, from the last upheaving start
Grass has died on grass in season, thorn had bred its counterpart.

Somewhere in that godless silence, python shivered in its sleep,
Leopard stirred and flexed and rippled off where shadows lay more deep.
Long giraffe must limberly have cantered then again made hush,
Deer and dikdik took more closely of the form of thorn and bush.
If the cactus glowed more pinkly it conveyed no moral tale -
In that land of lawless nature Aesop speaks to no avail:
The gargoyle branches sing of naught, the bloated baobab is dumb;
The noiseless people make their fetish with a primal goatskin drum.
Then the power of unrestricted nature pierced my shuttered mind,
As on wasteland moonlight's bounty had the thorn and rock refined;
And I could not hold the wonder and the beauty in my heart,
Finding room as well for slight - and so I bade the hurt depart.

Joyce Barton

BEYOND THE HORIZON

'Come' the chirpy morning called,
And gathering me with twinkling tenderness,
Swept me from the dewdrop land of freshness.

Warming in this embrace
I shed all personal preference
And let myself be led to a gentle millrace;
There a hail-whiteness dance
Intruded on the two-waters' silence
The face of the upper lake was smooth,
Enchanted mirror of my youth.

The lower lake, spreading out wider and wider,
Drank in high rocks, hillocks, dense foliage;
The air rose in greeting, expectant, keen,
And far away, an eye-beckoning panorama,
Grew grander, more mountainous,
No grassy plain was to be seen,
Hardly a land of milk and honey.

When I had selected a barque for my journey,
The wind whispered: 'Well chosen, bon voyage,
That boat has been named 'Self Knowledge'
I will blow you beyond the horizon.'

Mary Frances Mooney

THE CHERNOBYL DISASTER

Chernobyl in Russia is a small place,
Where disaster made people race,
A meltdown of nuclear station,
Was about to affect the entire nation.
The state of the station no one was told,
People of Chernobyl left out in the cold,
Corroded and decayed no alarm was sound,
Yet it blistered skin and poisoned the ground,
Radio active sickness of which we became aware,
But did anyone out there really care?
Many people were forced to mourn,
The tragic effect of the new and unborn,
Many left without a leg or arm,
Such a terrible thing did so much harm,
Many a life the disaster did shatter,
Words so difficult for people to utter,
They picked up the pieces and started again,
Still they live with the memory and pain,
It wasn't their fault they weren't to blame,
So who did it really put to shame?

Sally Ann Swain

GRUMBLE

We all like to grumble.
I suppose it keeps us sane.
All about the weather.
When it's fine we want rain.

We grumble about other people.
When they don't do what they should.
When we feel sick and poorly.
And things are far from good.

Yet I know a girl from Bosnia.
A war victim she did fall.
She was so hungry she ate the snow.
But she did not grumble at all.

Jenny Bosworth

BEYOND THE HORIZON OF LIFE!

Beyond the horizon of life my soul yearns to see
As out of this world we all have to flee!
If there's something beyond for you and for me
In a state of bewildered confusion are we
Is there someone out there to solve the mystery?
Our loved ones departed . . . to see them again . . .
A hint of a hope to ease the lingering pain!
To perceive a ghost . . . a ghost of chance
A phantom phantasm a little coherence
From Jerusalem, Lourdes, Mecca or Rome
No sign nor revelation of our final home
Strong be our faith . . . there's a niggling doubt
Perhaps a better world if figured out . . .?
No rhyme nor reason, fleeting lifetime's infernal
Just something concrete to prove it's eternal
An extraterrestre or angel devine . . .
An apparition or seer sublime!
A mystery unfolder for a boggled mind
A little consolation as the years grind
Is there someone out there who can tell us why:
Why do we live? Why do we die?
Our souls are afflicted with trouble and strife!
Is there something out there beyond the horizon of life?

Sheila Olivia Hogan

FACE AT THE WINDOW

Face looking out of the window
To catch the eye of anyone passing,
With a moment to spare.

Face looking out of the window
Hairy awry, wondering if there is food,
Thinking there is no money to buy.

Face looking out of the window
Turns to gently stroke a cat adopted,
Love and caressing accepted and enjoyed by both.

Face looking out of the window
Breaks into beautiful smiles when visitors arrive,
With food, cat food and ready prepared meals.

Face looking out of the window waving goodbye,
In minutes simply cannot remember,
If we have ever really been there.

Pauline Hamblin

ARMAGEDDON - BEYOND THE HORIZON

We were warned about greenhouse gases, but no-one took any heed.
Too busy working, making money, there didn't seem any need.
A big ship hit an iceberg, it shouldn't be off Dover.
Apparently others are in its wake, fifty yards wide or over.

The ozone layer has broken up, there's two or three big holes.
The arctic circles melting fast, there'll be some heavy tolls.
The gamma rays are getting through, warming up the land.
Suntan blocker ain't no good, it's getting out of hand.

Sea levels are rising every day, two feet more they say.
The landscapes changing drastically, nothing holds the sea at bay.
Some coastal roads have disappeared, streams are rivers too.
This is an emergency, someone must help, but who?

Pumping stations shutting down, contamination rife.
Is this our Armageddon? It's more than a bit of strife.
Trees and shrubs are dying, washed away by the tide.
The homeless head for higher ground, for somewhere dry to hide.

Food and water are getting short, lorries can't get through
Powergen have warned us all, major power failures due.
Radios working overtime, but time is running out.
This is disaster with a capital 'D', we couldn't handle drought.

Temperatures are soaring, it's 30°c in the shade.
People with fast motor boats, doing a ferrying trade.
What will be the end of this, millions of people dying.
Could the world have prevented this, to stem this tide, by trying.

The flotsam's unbelievable, when you reach the water line.
Wreckage and dead animals, sewage and green slime.
Holland's under water, London's underground is dead.
God my body's burning up, it's a dream, I'm in my bed.

B M Hurll

THE VOICE OF FAMINE

As you sit and eat your tea, think of me
As in your room you watch TV, think of me
In the morning as you arise in your nice warm bed
and rub your eyes, think of me
I have no food, no nice warm bed
No cosy place to lay my head
People around me are dying or dead
O how I wish they could have been fed
Please think of me.

S Y Lee

BEYOND THE HORIZON

When, on the wings of winds I soar;
higher than the highest heights;
the earth far beneath these wings
which carries me on;

Far into the horizon;
where snowflakes never cease
and the rays of the sun lightly kiss my lips
like the wings of a butterfly;
an array of beautiful colours meets my eye;
as far as I can see.

A realm I have never known
all around me;
enthralled I behold; a sight; far richer than gold;
my love for this realm grows
for this beautiful field of vision
within my reach.

Gladness fills my heart
my heart beats as loud sounds of drums
walking amongst the flower beds
inhaling sweet promises in the air
it's a feeling I cannot describe.

Birds of the air; flying in the horizon
beast of the fields through the twists of woods; I see
a bright light shining in the distance
beckoning to my very soul
the strangest feeling of peace fills my heart
I see the king of kings.

As I sweep nearer for to touch Him;
my eyes fluttered open; the vision fades away,
I lose the beautiful sight; beyond . . . far beyond the horizon.

Patricia Aboagye

LANCELOT'S PAIN

I wander destitute and lonely
across the empty wooded glade
wracked with feelings of guilt and pain
Guinevere, my forsaken paramour
Arthur, my Lord, my King, my friend
heart once pure, undefeated in combat
blessed by God's own light
all white, shining splendour
righteous and holy, my virtue unbounded
Queen's champion, to defend her name my calling
lured from the path, by lust and desire
a stolen snatched caress of angels
making my heart swell with joy
tasting of forbidden fruit
happiness short-lived
black shadow of discovery is cast
shamed, dishonoured
I stumble along the muddy forest track
lost in the turmoil of hate and anger
once proud knight
clad in tattered clothing, full of self-loathing
wounds inflicted upon the flesh
cannot mask the mental anguish of the deed committed
a breaking of vows
unintended, unforgivable yet unavoidable
memories awhirl, a maelstrom of confusion
the need to avenge my sins consumes remaining years
seeking redemption, repayment of my debt of honour
my only living purpose
forgive me my Liege.

Paul Birkitt

THE STAITHES

Wet wooden steps, moist and dank
climb down the slippery staithes
to the swirling flow of the tidal Trent

Piles of huge hulking timber
support the weaving wharf floor
projecting over the river gent

Cascading light falls sporadic
through narrow chinks above
sun-dappled water, belying danger

Black slimed pillars, shadow lurking
iron clamps, bolt-heads rusted red
in the dark, green weed spreads, river ranger

Relentless mat creeping across the silt
biting the ankles of wooden beams
damp smell of decay hangs in the air

Upon the broad staithe steps
town's people gather with jug and pail
fetching water for drinking and washing hair

Lovestruck single men proffer assistance
filling buckets for ladies in waiting
expecting little reward, a hand clasped with pleasure

Young sailors, their ships resting at anchor
carefully carry an attractive lady's pail
across three vessels or more, hugging tight their watery treasure

Scooping water where the river runs clean
one of many strange customs witnessed
by the silent staithes of Gainsborough town

Long since rotted and removed
dwelling in history, consigned to the past
lost in the mist of times veiled gown

Chris Bailey

STRANGE LAND

I am a granny, long past my exploring days,
But I feel the cold wind on my cheeks
As I lay in my tent with the wind howling
Across the tundra, and snow whipping up in peaks.
The sound of ice, cracking and groaning,
Wind moaning,
Tent flapping around me as I sit
Watching a single flame heat the soup,
Warming my blood, burning my lip.
Still days, snow glistening on frozen water
As I glide on my sled silently.
Huskies, straining to be first
To the pole, as I am, hopefully.
Giant chasms, deep, dark blue
High ridges of ice like teeth.
Like shifting sands the ice moves.
Fathoms of dark, cold water beneath.
The quiet and stillness of nothing,
Nothing that I could know,
The feeling of solitude and peace,
Strange, compelling land of ice and snow.

P Williams

A Transient Experience

I fell in love
with a woman on the train.
During our journey together
we lived a lifetime.
With each passing station
our affection grew.
As I looked into her eyes
before a background
of speeding landscapes,
I saw our future.
We were married in June.
We honeymooned and argued,
then danced at midnight.
On each anniversary
we kissed and remembered
the morning we first met.
Approaching my destination,
I saw an old couple.
A lifetime in love and finally . . .
bereavement.
A jolt marked my arrival
and with a final stare,
I blew a silent kiss to my widow
and wondered . . .
if we would ever meet again.

Shaun Kelley

Saga Of The Sunset

Who sails with me? far from this north wind land
Of ice and fire, whose steaming cauldrons boil
From hidden hell - the place of dark and light
Whose lissom demons leap into the night
To join the sun swept sky in whirling fantasy.

Who sails with me? away from sheltering shore;
Those lands explored hold no more stark surprise -
But through the mists, across the poisoned sea
There is another place, the sagas say,
Of fruited vines and gold and silver panoply.

Where dragons sport across an endless plain,
And tall trees grow whose branches touch the sky;
I sense this voyage is our destiny.
We leave our Viking lands where pillared ice
Stands crystalled sentinel of our domain.
The serpent ships, whose wombs will bear us all
Beyond the frontier of our ancient night-bound sand,
Dream silent, of their crunching hulls on alien strand.

We dare not seek to plunder this unknown,
So long elusive to mere human ken,
Whose women are the daughters of the stars -
Whose yielding to us still may prove us men.
If by the power of Odin we set sail,
Then in His wisdom let them be unfurled.
Around our dragon-prows the tides will stream
That have their bourne within another world.
Across our bows the sunset tints the spray,
A dancing mist veil of lightfeathered day.
The strength of gods is in my blood, a crimson sea -
I, Odin's son, repeat my cry: 'Who sails with me?'

Pamela Harvey

HOMELESS

I pray to God for forgiveness of my sins
And for help as I search yet more refuse bins.
I look and hope for crust to find
To keep the hunger from my mind.

A pedestrian speaks then passes by,
'Go home my friend before you die.'
Whose home, my home? What home and where?
I have no friend nor family who care.

I walk the streets with monotonous pace,
I yield to no one who enters my space.
For this is the world that I gave to me
Yet I know I am lost now I am free.

I know not where for help to turn,
For I am stubborn and never learn
From traumas suffered in my past,
That hurt me then but didn't last.

Without an address all work plans are lost,
So with a shrug, I pretend I don't care a toss.
Now I've been arrested for some small crime,
As I tried to end this life of mine.

It's six months later and they've let me go,
I look up at the sky and see that it's blue.
I walk to the church but the door is locked,
And realise my pathway to peace is blocked.

I know that I'm free of all crimes past,
And remember life isn't always to last.
So I spread my arms outward with soul intact,
And I scream to the world 'Homelessness is a fact'.

Kerry D Beck

BEYOND QUESTION?

Beyond this window, beyond that building,
Beyond this earth, beyond the sky,
I wonder, oh! I wonder
What is hidden from the human eye.

Beyond this sphere, beyond the star,
Beyond our sun, and moon, afar,
I wonder, oh! I wonder,
Just 'what' lies hidden there.

Beyond man's thoughts, beyond his ways,
Beyond man's tellings, and, songs of praise,
Beyond this life, beyond our world,
What lies I wonder -
What secret 'furled'?

Will 'I' the day that death calls find -
All answers to my questions, 'blind',
Might I glimpse, 'The Promised Lord'
Or, just within the ground be stored?

There to lie, to mould, to rot -
'Oblivious,' questioning not.

D Glossop

OUTER SPACE?

On the ceiling in my bedroom
In the corner dark and square
A piece of mesh boxed neatly
It's purpose - ventilation - air!

Yet there were two big windows
With three openings each
A door so ill fitting that one
Could limbo dance beneath!

Did we really need this air vent
So sinister, smug and black?
Sneering, staring down upon me
From the floor of the attic.

I covered my head with blankets
A small frightened child in a ball
Almost suffocated nightly
Less some Alien should call.

I never told my parents
But when I couldn't sleep
I'd call 'Goodnight' for hours
They'd reply 'Count sheep!'

Once I floated to the ceiling
Looking down upon my bed
Hovering weightless above it
They'd have said 'She's off her head!'

So I never told anyone till now
My scarlet hair, my funny face
The Aliens captured me I'm sure
Via the ceiling to Outer Space!

Margareth

THE DAILY ROUTINE

Peace the aspiration
War the routine of the day
Blood a common spillage
So the stain won't clean away

Soldiers on the streets
Their helicopters guard the sky
Some men are prepared to talk
And some prepared to die

Hatred is the daily bread
Each household gets a slice
They find it hard to swallow
But they pay the highest price

Cynicism flourishes
Suspicion leads the way
As Northern Ireland gets through
Yet another hectic day.

Kim Montia

GOD KNOWS

Maniacs and preachers
Churches and brothels
Computers and shovels
In the cybernetic-orchard,

Miracle cures
The saints and the sinners
The truth and fiction must collide
God knows turning the pages
Through the ages,

I've seen it all
From the other side,
God knows it's been fun.

K M Clemo

HIDING FROM CONFLICT

Transparent flame flickering
Yellow into fearful eyes,
Lighting dark faces to waxen pale,
Swirling threads of vapour shadow
Coiling from wicks of twisted rushes
Soaked in heavy acrid tallow.

Aged ancients, women, children,
Hunched in the murky glow
Of the hidden cave,
A subterranean world of chambers,
Listening to the outside conflict
Of fighting men and marauders.

From the nearby village
The bitter sulphurous taint of smoke
Rising from their homes -
They stared into the bright flame curling
In spirals from the flare of rushes,
Fluttering the wild shadows dancing.

E Francis

REACHING FOR PERFECTION

Reaching for perfection;
Then life is over
In a brief sigh or breath,
Watching a dapple of sunlight
On fragile autumn leaves,
Or gently touching
A baby's hand,
Or water over grey-green stones,
Ripples of enchantment,
Here, then gone in an instant,
A moment of Eternity,
Captured in a frieze
By knowing eyes,
Then flowing on -
The flight of the soul
To another land.

Peter Corbett

DEATH FOR A TUSK

On the surface of this broth of heat
floats the acrid stench of death.
Game-warden curses his long defeat,
whilst I gag, and catch my breath.

Before long, Askari wave a sign,
crouching as they part the grass.
Soon, I find my eyes with tears are blind -
stricken by the butchered mass.

Self-consciousness at own sweaty scent
forgotten in this presence.
I always thought I knew what was meant
by 'waste' - that notion's past tense!

Once huge, majestic, bull elephant -
now . . . mere carrion! Tragic
that callous greed driven miscreants
deprived us of this magic!

Phoenix Martin

Dartmoor Prison (Beneath Your Mist)

Cold kissed blank mist
Completely blanket this blot,
Cover well this grey granite sight
Of Dartmoor's unsightly face,
So none may tell.
Hide for shame this house of numbers
Of countless men without a name,
Conceal their lack of hope
Hopeless to reveal,
The truth at best be stifled
Suffocated under a vapoured air.
Stillness changes not the time
Of timeless souls astir,
Except to those whom care.
Chilly ghosts of a past forgotten
Who stone by stone built this icy tomb,
American and French prisoners of war
In their bondage of 1805,
It was a good year for the empire
Or so we all were told.
They built with bleeding hands acold
And clotted empty bellies raw,
Belay they now where well fed dogs patrol
Within the sterile zone,
Bleached against a crumbling wall
Of mildew, moss and bone,
Yet still bonded to the system's control.
So seal tight you mists, don't lift,
And of the ghosts whom haunt this place,
Leave them and I alone.

Norman Royal

TO BE ANOTHER LIFE FORM

To be a leaf and to unfurl,
High up in the canopy of a rain-forest,
Where monkeys gather wide eyed and mischievous,
And where the blue sky peeps,
Through gathered branches,
To feel raindrops for the first time,
As they roll across my surface and fill each crevice and fine line,
Then fulfilling destiny,
To wither and fall twisting and twirling,
Until I weave into the carpet on the forest floor,

To be a beautiful flower bursting forth,
In colour rich,
Whose petals open to the sun,
And sway gently in the breeze,
Where butterfly alight,
Dressed in their finest array,
A union of beauty merging,
And departing as they flutter away,
Until my petals reach to the sun one last time,
Then one by one fall to nature's carpet on the forest floor,

To be a feather in the plumage of a tropical bird,
In flight as it soars on high and skims the trees,
In unison with the sky,
To glide streamlined with outstretched wings,
In shades of indigo and green of metallic hue,
To feel the air rush by this aerial master,
Of his craft in flight,
And feel the warmth of the enclosed beating heart,
Then one day to float at random loose and free,
A merging pattern in the carpet on the forest floor.

Ann G Wallace

From The Desert

There is little to say about dying.
No relief in the dry
Hot sun of the day
After cold night.
Hopeless
The tight skin,
The weak pulse within.
And never one drop,
One blessed drop to stop
Everything withering,
Everything shrivelling
Into dust -
Bright eye,
Loved one
Into hot dust.

Alasdair Aston

COME BE SET FREE

His light His might
Piercing darkness
Through His light. His might
Our foundations crumbling
Fountains cascading, tumbling, squirling
Smashing barriers, defences, all reality, all time.
Breaking through self's dust and grime.
Now gushing from the throne
Gifts of love, peace, joy to every man, woman, girl, boy.
Setting us free from past generations' pain
We can receive and His glory gain.
Grasp, lay hold of His truth welcome the King of Glory in
Let Him burn, peel off the layers of sin.
In the furnace bubbling, rumbling,
Melting all dross brought to the surface
Hearts breaking, souls refined, made whole.
Come now, it's free, for all. God's Spirit loves to impart
Gifts of love to a contrite heart, that's full of unquenched thirst,
Overflows, then bursts into rivers gives all uncrucified flesh the shivers.
As the sun warms the frozen ground,
Love tests, then God's precious grace
And mercy with love abounds.
Now we've liberty and joy pressing through
Able labourers in God's employ.
Not under man's law as we empty ourselves
Of all bitterness and hurt,
Having kicked out past generations' curse
Wanting to tap into that everlasting stream
To quench some thirst.
The cost is dour but spirit-flesh can't stay sour,
Eaten alive to the core, no longer bleeding and sore,
Crying out for more.

Not expecting thanks but to our one true God
Have our spirit, soul and body quenched.
Being filled with all desires of heart,
We lay down our wills, and fleshly skills,
For a lost and dying world
God's life giving Spirit to impart.

Lesley J Worrall

ONCE AND FOREVER

Do you recall the Flying Boats that flew from Oban Bay,
The spinning wave, the roar that sent an echo through the dawn,
The flashing lamp, a hand that waved, the long slow rise that
                                                                curved -
Ah, all of that, my love, is gone as is our yesterday.

The months they flew, my love, the years that went to mark
                                                                   our life,
The fogs, the rain, the winds that blew like knives from
                                                              out the North -
I hear it still, that roar that went an-echoing down the loch,
In dreams, in memories still, my love, of that long-vanished strife.

The bay is quiet now, my love, its yachts are bright and gay,
And children play where once a plane lay shattered on the strand,
And there the Asdic flashed its light and gunfire rattled sharp -
But ah, my love, all that is just our long-gone yesterday.

Dorothea Gray

LIBERATION

When our earthly shell's been shed
Free from illness, cares and woes,
No more tossing in our bed,
Wracked with pain, now all that goes.

Spirit here midst early strife,
Now spirit there without form,
We now live another life,
Safe from harm, secure and warm.

What a truly wondrous sight
To see and know guides and friends,
Bathed in love and pure white light,
God's great wonder never ends.

With our dear ones who have passed
Now on a new vibration,
Peace and joy and freedom at last,
Now this is liberation.

Suzanne Joy Golding

UNTITLED

My Voice   *Her Voice*

I am your sister
I shared the womb.

                    My sister is dying
                    We'll soon share a tomb.

I am your mother
I gave you birth.

                    My mother is lying
                    Bones on the parched earth.

I am your daughter
Hold me tight

                    My daughter is clinging
                    She can't stand upright.

                    My body is yours
                    But for a slight twist of fate
                    My hopelessness too
                    For I know it's too late
                    For hell is to hold
                    The one you love best
                    A hungry child
                    To an empty breast
                    There must be a reason
                    But as hunger gnaws
                    I am fading away
                    The answer must be yours

                    My sister

                    My mother

                    My daughter.

Katy Plant

THE GATHERING

Swirl of blackness fills the sky
squabbling, swooping
black-fingered vultures circling high
white ruffled neck feathers
stabbing beak, twinkling eye
hopping closer, acting brave
strutting talons, squawking cry
picking flesh, scavenged bones
dust of time passes by
unwanted companions standing vigil
patiently waiting for them to die
harassing hunters
watching dying breath softly sigh
flocking, sound of the grave
perched still with features sly
fighting, brawling
long neck stretching, the end is nigh
undertaker of the plains
death's ambassadors in ambush lie

Luke Thomas

LIVING AMONGST THE LAND MINES
(In memory of Chris Howes)

Who really cares about the third world child,
That plays on the wasteland, or maybe runs wild,
Yesterday he was a solitary figure, kicking about an old tin can,
Unaware in complete oblivious innocence,
Of the land mine planted in the couch grass,
By its thoughtless, ruthless creator, man,
Obsessed by war, the rebel's heart for compassion, cannot transpire,
Those limbs were trapped between the concealed wire,
Who has the right to torture and maim,
An orphaned child that maybe cannot even spell his name,
No mummy or daddy to hug him or kiss him good-night,
No artificial legs or crutches will put this wrong right,
Past wars have shown, the world is to blame,
So please reflect before you place the next land mine,
If not bow your guilty head in shame.

C Beodricksworth Reynolds

NIA-TAMA'S CHILDREN - RWANDA

Black flies constantly singing
to the children of Nia-Tama,
Their noise brings no comfort,
While soft tears and runny noses
are spots where the singing flies can drink.
Sleep keeps out the pain, morning does not
break at the crowing of the cock.
The first gunshot wakes everyone, putting them
back, keeping them here with the crack of the shot.
Nia-Tama's children wake up crying and
the black flies, once again, start singing.
Just like the day before, and the day before that,
and the day before that.
Yes, and the day before that.

Antony Gilbert

THE SPIRIT WITHIN

If I look into a mirror,
and pass a thought or two,
is there any evidence
that God's alive in me?

When I see the setting sun,
or marvel at the dew,
do I see a blade of grass,
and wonder whence it came?

The skipping lamb bears testament,
of nature's springtime joy,
budding flowers, kittens too,
all are welcomed with wide eyed awe.

Walk along the country lanes,
see the hedgerows open eyed,
not by chance or accident,
does Mother Nature nurture so.

Open up your eyes to sights,
of more beauty than man's plans,
only God, his palette primed,
produces colours so vivid and pure.

Now I know the answer too,
He must be living, He must be here,
He's in my heart, He's in my eyes,
He paints His picture, He lets me in.

Paul Wadge

AFTERNOON TEA

It rained today,
It rains every day in the monsoon season,
I find it soothing.

But not today,
Today, we had a tropical storm,
Wow! The lightning.

What a day,
The lightning struck our pylon,
It was frightening.

Fans like dervishes,
Electric appliances gone mad,
No ironing.

Wishing I had!
Mrs Wong shouts down to me,
'Tea's brewing.'

M C Taylor

Space

We are saying,
Goodbye to our earth,
Flying past the moon.
To the stars,
You are smiling Mother Earth.
We will return from the sky.
Our future out in the universe,
Out into the Milky Way,
We will fly into space,
To race with time.
Goodbye earth
The planet of our birth
Here we come universe
Beyond the earth's horizon
In the twilight zone
A long way from home,

Land on one of them twinkling diamonds.
See a horizon of a different dimension.

B Clarke

Afternoon Tea

It rained today,
It rains every day in the monsoon season,
I find it soothing.

But not today,
Today, we had a tropical storm,
Wow! The lightning.

What a day,
The lightning struck our pylon,
It was frightening.

Fans like dervishes,
Electric appliances gone mad,
No ironing.

Wishing I had!
Mrs Wong shouts down to me,
'Tea's brewing.'

M C Taylor

SPACE

We are saying,
Goodbye to our earth,
Flying past the moon.
To the stars,
You are smiling Mother Earth.
We will return from the sky.
Our future out in the universe,
Out into the Milky Way,
We will fly into space,
To race with time.
Goodbye earth
The planet of our birth
Here we come universe
Beyond the earth's horizon
In the twilight zone
A long way from home,

Land on one of them twinkling diamonds.
See a horizon of a different dimension.

B Clarke

NUTRITION FOR YASHODA

The crowd wait with rewards
For a long wrinkled branch
To trumpet in triumph.
The stone walls are high
And strong enough to comfort
The most timorous hand.

Once, in a bleak French cave
We stood in awe before
A great woolly mammoth.
The drawing was stunning
It echoed of divine worship.
A million years on . . .

Yashoda's dark eyes blink,
Another camera must capture
Their brave little rider.
I want her to rage
Use the power of India
Instead of just quietly dying.

She's caught in a land
Of white winter dreams.
After twenty odd years
Her weather-beaten trunk
Drinks deep to remember,
Water bursting from the Ganges.

Maureen Macnaughtan

BEXHILL STREETS AFTER SCHOOL

St Richard's pupils were waiting for my train,
Soon to be theirs, Hastings-bound with well learnt patience -
That's more than I could say for inmates of other schools,
Who would not have behaved so well at stations.
They murdered old people's patience, just like buffoons -
In Sea, and Endwell Roads, daring each other,
With skateboards and mountain bikes. Their peccadilloes
Could earn them a name like 'Bexhill Desperadoes'.

Glyne Gap Cafe had been dumb, while the south coast sun shone
Till its young patrons rode in, to prevail upon
The ice-cream seller, for cones and Soleros
To keep them cucumber-cool. (That day was torrid.)
Educational jails couldn't be more horrid.
Sea-crazy pals carried towel and costume Swiss rolls
In hopes of practise - to score gala-racing goals.

Gillian C Fisher

BLINDED BY THE LIGHT

The wind is whistling through the trees,
Causing nothing but a slight breeze,
Travelling down the windy lane,
Going nowhere in vain,
Turning round corner after corner,
This place is getting foreigner and foreigner,
Nightfall is slowly beginning to fall,
The owls have stirred, they're starting to call,
What and why am I doing here?
The dream's slowly, vaguely beginning to reappear,
My life's flashing before my very eyes,
Until then I never realised,
The night before I actually died,
Today they've gathered together and cried,
I'm travelling, solemnly towards the light,
My soul tugging at strings to make it right,
Suddenly I'm looking down into the room,
Looking at the clock, I recalled it was noon,
Fast asleep I seemed to be,
Lying so still, is that really me?
All of a sudden, I wake up with a start,
Clasping my hands quickly to my heart,
Am I still here
Or am I there?
Blinded by the light streaming through the panes,
Rising up, I'm travelling towards the windy lanes,
Stepping forward, then spun around,
Slowly being lowered to the ground,
Peace?

Sonia Conway

INFORMATION

We hope you have enjoyed reading this book - and that you will continue to enjoy it in the coming years.

If you like reading and writing poetry drop us a line, or give us a call, and we'll send you a free information pack.

Write to :-
**Triumph House Information
1-2 Wainman Road
Woodston
Peterborough
PE2 7BU
(01733) 230749**